I0380323

Previous Publications:

Born, Black Stone Press, 1975

Handbook of Ornament, Black Stone Press, 1979

The Gospel of Mary, Woodley Press, 1997

god won't overlook us, Penthe Press, 2001

Abundance, 219 Press, 2004

Voice Over, Blue Cedar Press, 2012

And So it Goes, Blue Cedar Press, 2014

The Comedic Applicant, Blue Cedar Press, 2015

The Average Level of Happiness, Blue Cedar Press, 2016

Human Ink: The First Five Books, Blue Cedar Press, 2017

Ain't Leavin' This House Rough-Dried, Spartan Press, 2019

An Incident That Might Lead To Something,
Spartan Press, 2020

YOU MUST HAVE YOUR FAMINE

Poems by Michael Poage

Spartan Press

Kansas City   Missouri

Spartan Press

Kansas City, MO

spartanpress.co

Spartan
Press

Acknowledgments:

Gasconade Review: "Tiger, Tiger," "Evening News," "The Spider."

TABLE OF CONTENTS

I. WHERE ARE MY CHILDREN?

II.   SCOTTISH PRAYER BOOK

III.   SCRAPE

To Edward Goode, who, without taking the authoritative designation, "Godfather," away in any sense from A., has come to take on that role for so many of us in this family. And early on he heeded the words: "You are the salt of the earth;" "You are the light of the world."

THE WOMAN:

Kiss me—full on the mouth!
Yes! For your love is better than wine,
Headier than your aromatic oils.
The syllables of your name murmur like a meadow's brook.
No wonder everyone loves to say your name!

-Song of Songs, 1:2-3, The Message
Peterson translation

WHERE ARE MY CHILDREN?

"IF THIS ENDS"

If this ends   will we
   still be friends (question)

Probably not (answer)   That makes me sad (statement)

Why (question)   I will miss you (answer)

It will be impossible (statement)   Why (question)

It will be too painful (answer)   For you (question)

No, for you (answer)

MISSING

Where are my children?
They were with me
when we all
went to sleep at dark
last night. I've been
going mad for years
in fear this kind of thing
would happen.

But what is "this kind of thing"?
Any minute now
I will lean out this window
of my apartment
and scream for the five of them:
Listen. You were with me at dark.

WAITING, WANTING,

Waiting, wanting,
standing, storming.
The pain
has been strong
since coming back
from the bridge.
This is
not an apology.
I am one
of the last
to use film,
even black and white.
On the bridge
I decided
just a few
more photos.

SANTA MONICA

We could not
Stand each other
For one more meal
Or television show,
Another sweet smile
Smothered in gravy
Or traffic jam
The length of 10
From Santa Monica
To wherever it finally
Finds allelulla freedom,
Which, as Janis Joplin
Reminded us, is just
Another word for
Nothing else to lose.

RETURN FLIGHT

baby, it's cold
outside
i know
you really
must go
i just want
to say
we should try
one more
time

time
is with us
we can keep
warm

warm
is with us
more time
more time
more time
round trip

MARRIAGE

Walking the river
With the wind coming
From the usual south
The ripples of surface
Water go the way
Of the wind – disguised
As rushing north.
But the deep wellship
Of the river flow
Is moving otherwise
In opposition to
The blind world so
Angry at the filthy
Truth that sets
The river free
To flood at will.

LOVER

The fabric tulip
keeps its shape
long into the
winter. I do
well remember
holding your face
in my hands
gentle as a lover
and I so well
remember your
soft line of
skin along the
cheek bone on each
side of your face.
Believe me, when I
say, you were the only
one? I know of
your skeptic nature,
full embrace coming
so absent of abandon.

YOUNG BRIDE

The bride, so young,
in her white dress,
could not speak
but only squealed
nervous laughter
as we gathered at the
front of the sanctuary.
This was her day
between the high notes
of her musical fear
when the taking of a
breath brought silence.
She prayed for hope
that the sacred vow
would break through
the terror of losing
it all, her whole life,
to a handsome violence
that would make her
scream and twist
until her last laugh
and her final breath
forced blood stains
on that white dress.

LAST KISS

I remember Karen Lynch.
But I probably should not use her
Name like this in public. Wait!
This is a poem, no one in the public domain
Will read it so her name won't become an instant
Household word. There's no fear of libel.
Like I was saying, I remember Karen Lynch.
Nineth grade. Kansas. She was beautiful,
Too beautiful for me. Me, too shy for her.

What I don't remember is how I was talked
Into asking her to the movies, or how
I got up the courage to put my arm
Over her shoulders in the dark of the back row,
Or how we turned to each other
At the exact same moment, accidentally
Brushing our lips softly together, like a
southern summer breeze that, all of a sudden,
Turns from the north signaling violence.

FLOOR

There is often
that tension over
speaking or not
when you are half over
me and covering my
face with
kisses. We are trying
to recover something in
our lives. And as with
many people it is
awkward. I feel a dull
ache in the pelvic floor –
like an open mouth
wanting to scream
but failing. I remember
now the untangling
of our legs
and arms, a clumsy
caress of my breast,
or maybe it was my face.
And I know you recall
how we stood carefully,
not looking into
each other's eyes,
we embraced
as one ex to another.

BODY UNIDENTIFIED

You drift closer to
the mainland. Low
flying airplanes and
boats of various sizes
search from the sky
and the surface spotting
illusions of hope for
your life. Nameless
you float with the
ebb of the tide and
the pull of the moon.
You are a creature
of the sea having made
a lifetime for the
world's survivors to
search out. Even if
discovered the naming
will be impossible
as no one will dare come
forward to claim you.

THE POND AND THE TEAL

The pond has a heart
And it throbs loud
And steady for the teal.
It is July and years
Since the breaking up
Of a love lyric with
Smiles anyone passing by
Would recognize as fragile
Like the gold leaf around us.
The teal and the pond are
Beautiful in this photo
Taken around the same time
As they fantasized a life together.

PLAYING IT SAFE

Out of the corner of your eye
You see an ad on television
For a video game. All you see
Are the words: Play your heart out.
But you are already
Standing on the edge
With little heart left
For more risk-taking.
You have asked your
Therapist about some way
To put your heart in a cast
To help the healing. She replies,
It is not a bone, how would
It work? You reply, You are wrong,
My heart is bone, not flesh, not
A muscle, therefore it does
Not tear, it breaks.
And it is a compound fracture.
So, please, wrap it in cloth
And plaster, let it dry.
Someone may want to sign their name.

DYING FOR LOVE

Does he talk about
what he believes?
No. Just wanting
the angels to come
and take him. Sounds
like belief to me. Yes?
I'm told you can
make money with aloe plants.
You have to find the right
people to buy them.
The bigger the plant
the more buyers will spend.
Do they believe in the healing?
Whether angels or aloe
we come to the same
desert expanding on its own
and changing the nature
of the beautiful continent.
Dust becomes us and
the earth tumbles into
the lush green of our
love. Pulling the sheets up
over us we can laugh
and be buried at the same time.

AMICABLE

There was this road
traveling the river.
Sooner, rather than later,
they argued. Even the
tallest of the old trees
trembled as the raging
continued. Winter after
winter, season from season,
the road and the river
threw bad names and
rocks at each other.
I remember this as a
child. I am still haunted
by the sight of empty
stream beds, small trees
terrified to grow to fullness,
and even what were the high
grasses stunted by neglect
and hate. I witnessed this
death and you were
with me. We both starved
and, even in our anger, we
could not destroy each other.

FIRST KISS

Often during the night
I hear only the sound
of the neighbor's television.
The words all run
together, melting into
one long monologue
of chatter with a
scream or a shout
to occasionally interrupt
the drivel. Now, there's a word
we don't see every day!
It's like a discovery for
this special moment. Like
moving my hand up a
very smooth and naked
leg, the first kiss of
love-falling, during the night,
often, I hear only the sound.

LOOSE CHANGE

We met for coffee
at a large bookstore.
I was standing in front
of the Lonely Planet guides
when you came up behind me.
I felt the light touch
of your breasts through
your blouse and my shirt
against my back and your face
resting on the pillow
between my shoulder blades.
I know your smile
gave the security
cameras something to talk about
when they finished
their shift and went wherever
security cameras go
for rest and a good meal.
Then you slipped your hands
into my front pants pockets.
You were not searching
for nickels or dimes.

THE SPIDER

You make it sound so easy.
Then you change your mind
And bring the argument into
Focus from a different
Angle. You don't notice
The black spider walking
Along the edge of your
Coffee cup. The discussion
Continues – mostly on
The literary merits of a full
Stop. But you forget about
The war around us,
The anger and fear
Striking like lightning
Ourselves and our neighbors.
The world knows nothing,
Cares less. You could
Put your hands gently
On the side of my face
Only for the sake of affection.
The spider is oblivious,
Spins a web across your cup.

TIGER, TIGER

What is intimate to you
Is only what gets caught
In your teeth. It takes
Practice to do what you do
With such skill. The play
With siblings in childhood,
Faking a throat-grab then
A sharp snap at the rump
Is only a prelude to the love
Of the kill that will come
Sooner than I ever imagined.
You're down on your stomach
In the brown grass with more
Patience than you can keep
Hidden. You move toward your
Prey before your instinct would
Allow so you know it's a mistake
From the start. I see what
You are doing so I lunge
Out of the reach of your
Lecherous, poor-excuse-for-claws
Attack and you tumble away
Out of view, over the steep cliff,
Dropping out the window on the
Twentieth floor and land on
The pavement, the sweet savanna
Twisted and contorted in more
Erotic ways than you can picture
On the pavement, the sweet savanna.

EVENING NEWS

It was a blood moon
but the news reporter
said: "Blue moon." She
never corrected herself.
This Tuesday was a beautiful
spring day but the
news reporter cautioned
us, saying, there are
reports of possible severe
storms from the
southwest. She continued
with how cool dry air
would or 'could' meet with
warm moist air
right over our state.
Stay tuned, she warned.
I considered the Percocet
left over from a recent
hospital visit. There is an
enjoyable high from the
narcotic but also the usual
caution about addiction and,
since that runs in my
family, I decided to heed
the warning. I waited for
the next blue moon, severe storms.
I am staying tuned in.

WINTER FORECAST

The newspaper forecast
is for a lot of snow
this year. It would be
unusual in this part of
the Great Plains. I could
be expected to dream
about the ice you
have melted with your
body near mine. It is
a life-saving trick
when stranded by a
blizzard. Take off our
clothes, each of us,
crawl into the sleeping bag
skin to skin. If we are lucky
the body warmth will help
us survive the coldest night.

HARVEST

We have to do something
With the tomatoes. It was
Thirty-seven degrees last night.
The image falls on the retina,
For her – a membrane of despair.
We have to do something.
She cannot keep holding her knees
Up to her head and feel comforted.
It is time for the harvest,
Salvage everything now or nothing
Will get us through the winter.
Even the slope of the roof looks
Unprepared for the snow to come.
The whole house looks sad
And frightened by the coming
Weather. The dogs already
Are spending nights in the haystacks
Building their bodies with warm
Blood while they have nightmares,
Barking and whining in their sleep.

THE NEW

The new moon, meaning
No moon that I can see,
Could be blood red or yellow
As dying leaves. Come and go
Radiating or in silence
With your body across mine
I imagine, remember, the bombing
Of the city and waiting for so much
To happen in our lives
And waiting and waiting
Finally gathering it all with us
For that one year of care,
Caress and love the color
Of leaves or the moon bleeding.

WILLOW WEEP

as you always do no matter
what the occasion, magnitude,
or tiny sad delay in our lives.
Still you have that same chronic
stoop of the shoulders while your
many limbs drag along the sidewalk,
wave with the breeze to the sway
of history. On this date in 1812
Beethoven wrote a passionate letter
to an unknown woman. Don't we all?

THE OTHER WOMAN

You would be hard to explain.
You come in and stand, walk around,
in and out the door. You go to the
playground.

Be careful. Watch your step. You go to the swing.
Up and back, into the air. You try to fly out of the way.

PANSION STARI GRAD

Juliet, Juliet, that is the hurting part.
You wake up
and in the mirror
see your life
only
in black and white.
Juliet, that is the hurting part.
It's a life-threatening situation for those of you
living north of Paradise, praying in Nebraska. Juliet
open your eyes
as you wake up
see yourself
in black and white.
Your life
depends on it, north of Paradise, the hurting part.
Juliet, Juliet,
and it's grown to be
a life-threatening situation for
those of you under siege in Stari Grad, across the ocean
from Paradise, that is the hurting part,
open your eyes, see the blackbirds, thirteen
of them only in black and black
you wake up.
Your life depends
on it, the situation

threatening Paradise,

Juliet, Juliet, you are

not invited to the party, open your eyes to the life-

threatening possibilities north of Paradise.

Juliet, Juliet, that is the hurting part.

SCOTTISH PRAYER BOOK

HISTORY OF SCOTLAND

You walk along the beach
with the angled stones,
huge flat rocks, sliding
out of the water and sand
but not moving, dead still.
You balance from one ancient
massive miracle to another
daring any one of them to
throw you into the water but
you are conquering all of
nature and your own worry
about leaving the beach
and going back to the house.
The danger in small rooms
shows on your salted face.
Your tight fist, another
example of a geological
work of god, also the size
of your pounding heart,
also the only way to
make your life a choice
fighting through the muir,
the moor, the Scottish history
of never quite breaking away
in spite of spears, drums and
pipes. Cold sea water offers
the escape of drifting away.

CUPID AT THE NORTH SEA

I am leaning toward giving up.
Perhaps it's hormones or just
Getting older, losing confidence
Or interest. No, not losing interest.
There are times when I feel the wave
Of desire and I am encouraged. I see
Someone's smile to me and mine to her.
Someone's smile to me and mine to her.

I recently read an article in the AARP
Magazine about Cher: She says:
"I'm not stepping aside, yet." But I
Am not Cher. And I am not dead!
I'll continue to enjoy those smiles and
The wave of desire with its sea salt taste.

TRAIN TO EDINBURGH

Scotland, 2014

Our next stop is Dundee.
It is a point of change
For many going to Glasgow
Or other towns surrounded
By sheep and bales of hay.
You sit across the aisle,
Facing each other, the table
Between you. You face
Opposite directions. One of you
Reads but you look out
The window as if praying
Or planning. You're walking
The beach across from Fife
Holding hands, kissing the bite
Of her lips, crazy in love.
You glance at the sky,
Catch your breath in the surprise
Of love-making reflected
In the window of the train.
Holding you close, she
Asks you not to cry in front
Of everyone. She says,
Catch your breath, and read.

AUBADE

It's French for dawn so start
with a bright morning.
Uncover your head to the sky
and clear the fight
from your eyes. Bless the
small flowers under your bare
feet and wash from your memory
the tides of St. Monan's.
Fire is in the stove, the black
dirt will swell the seed
to growth for a second cutting.
Tears are too wet to help
and the salt will dry white on your
boiled face eyeing the sea.

MY BEAUTIFUL PUB

The ale has every intention
Of frothing over the lip
For a chance
To have her fingers
Caress the foam
And the glass.
She reads the language
Of the grasses
Coming out of the Borders.
Night in the valley
Gives way to
The blues playing
In the only coffee shop
Among the few
Homes left living
The seclusion
Along the shallow
River Tweed.
Even the clouds
Cannot keep
Their secrets knowing
She is watching the sky
With the black of her eyes.

BBC ALBA

The dark place of the past
two weeks has been choking
you like the brogue or brick
on the coast near Cullen.
The farther north we come
the more solid the call for
independence . That is why I
came here, as close to the rock
edge as I've been in years.
Now feel how much is love, how
much is cleaning up the mess.

LEAVING HEATHROW

We begin to fly over
the North Atlantic
and immediately
encounter turbulence
which halts
the beverage service.

I fall asleep
imagining the disappearance
of my pension
and Social Security.
I don't like political dreams.
I fall from grace, actually
I jump. It is a slow
decline like the decent
into Chicago. I have been
cleared to land
and disguise my dreams.
More turbulence.

DUNNOTTAR CASTLE, STONEHAVEN, ABERDEENSHIRE

Fate is sealed with the North Sea
On one side and Cromwell's army
On the other – there is more to this
Than meets the eye – the "aye" –
Yes! And a double Scotch to calm
The nerves of combat. Take
The crown jewels for instance,
No, really, take them and
Hide them so they
Disappear for decades.
Maybe someone will find
Them in a trunk or something.
There is more than meets
The eye. Yes! Look into mine.
I have not felt this way
In decades. I want
To laugh. I want to believe
There is hope, like the tide
Filling the harbor forever.

BEGGAR'S BELIEF

*

The roads are wet with the October rain
and I walk. Keep walking. The sea to the north ends
in ice. In ancient stories, the gods send storms from the north.
"This crazy weather," they say here in Moray,
"wait five minutes and it will change."
I hear the same in Kansas.

*

I have not written much about you
so I will be direct: You were my nephew,
my sister's son, sent to me by our mother when you were eight.
She hoped I would calm the storm already stirring
inside you, put you on the magical yellow brick
road leading to the Emerald City.
Instead you stole auto repair tools from
the hardware store next door
hoping to take them back home to California
to please your dad. That would be
for you, the Emerald City, to give
your dad something he needed
and he would be glad, and he would
hug you and say, Evan, I love you.

*

I could only find you a not-so-magical
dirt road. You discover all the rents,
stones and ragged-edged holes
and you fell head first.

                    *

The call came from your stepdad.
Your girl friend returned the ring.
Standing in the restaurant parking lot
you put the .45 to your head, the one in your dad's
truck, his gun, at twenty-four.

It's a dirt road
around your whole body.
Head first.

                    *

The storm waves crash on the rocks
washing your feet. The wind is being
it's stormy self, still angry at you.
Interesting that your name means rock.
You have anchored yourself at the edge of the world,
standing tall, you beg the arctic ice
to come closer
because now you believe, ashes and all.

GORILLA COFFEE

Looking across Princes Street
I see the contemporary art
Building and above it,
Edinburgh Castle.

Wars rage, ISIS threatens
The world, my wife is
Buying a few clothes
To replace the ones

In her lost luggage.
"25 Years of Contemporary
Art in Scotland," features
The Art of Golf.

I will not go there.
But I will finish
My coffee called:
Gorilla Coffee. Beans

From Rwandan farmers
To help lift them out
Of poverty. A family laughs.
They are not from Rwanda.

CULLEN SKINK

One morning, my Texas
granddaughter, on her way
to first grade observed:
"Rules are…
unattractive."

I recall this as I walk
down North High Street,
Portsoy, Banffshire,
wishing she was with me.
We would meet many

dogs and people would
let us walk their dogs
like we did in Austin
last July. Luisa!!
Your name would be

a good one for Scotland
although it's a long way
from home here at the edge
of the world. But I know
you would understand

you do not have to taste
my bowl of skink, you can choose
macaroni and cheese instead.
It would also help if you would hold
my hand as my world becomes
less and less like yours.

SCOTTISH SONNET

Each day is different.
I have to spend time here
Close to the sea stacks
Of red and black sandstone
Moving into and out of
The quiet North Sea imagining
A tide. Fool the life
Of all identity.

Waves carry the spirit
From me to you over
The years, the miles.
It costs so much,
"it" being what is given
In the stone and the buried.

AFFECTION

On the train to Aberdeen
The young woman, travelling
With her boyfriend, was
Reading a book: I LOVE DICK.
The young man was also reading
But I could only see a part
Of the cover. It was an American
Flag but instead of stars in the blue
There were small Nazi symbols.
I wanted to talk, discuss
The books but in the midst of their reading
They were being very affectionate
With each other. I did not want
To bother them. A small table
Separated us so it was difficult
Not to watch their enjoyment
Of each other. I tried to bury myself
In my own book by Lahiri: THE LOWLAND.
Subhash and Holly were just getting
To know each other. He began
Staying at her small house when
Her son, Joshua, stayed the weekend
With his father. I read about
Their enjoyment of each other.

FIBER

I expected you would say that.
Not because I am psychic
But only watching as the North Sea
Pounds the brains of this planet
With wisdom and we do not
Embrace the love of salt
And muscle. We hand over
The fiber of our souls
To some insane, lost god,
Without the faintest hope
Of gathering the battered
Night-sound of seedlings
Betrayed by the very soil
Meant to be our home.

ORKNEY'S

You have your teeth
Back and it feels so much
Better. You return to
Tearing apart your
Rare beef steak
And pound the table
With guttural abandon.
The little ones watch
With no worry
For their own lives
As long as you remain
Where you are with teeth
Locked into muscle
And flesh like the iron
Jaws of the trap
Sprung in time, just
In time, to save
John Groat from the
Imprisoned faces of grief,
Island to island.

TAKE YOUR SCOTTISH LIFE

Stand close to the ocean home.
You can close your right hand into a fist.
Love the waves breaking over your out-stretched arm.
You are the only one who goes this far into the North Sea.
That is not true. Others go to great lengths

To take their lives far out to sea,
Drop them like an anchor.

SCOTTISH SONNET #8 (CROVIE)

If we had a king size bed
We could go all day and night
Without touching each other.
It would be the size of a country,
Twice as large as a desert.
I've been told I can be annoying.
Spare the change and bring me the rest
Before nightfall. I have friends

In low places I never knew about.
They will watch over me and not just
This one time but forever or as long as I live.
From this high up you can see all the houses
I stormed out of, the waves so strong I'll never
Ever dare again to trouble the waters.

"LADE"

(Scot's for: channel of water)

I suppose I've mentioned
wanting to see your horses
because I want to see you.

And perhaps I asked about
your daughter because I like
to see your face when you speak

of her. She has so much courage,
you say. I say, I believe she
got that trait from you. I linger

at the door convinced of the safety
of being near you and talking.
Sometimes you have put your

hand on my arm before I open
the door to leave. Always, I hope
for my own courage until next time.

THE CLIFFS OF MOHER

Ireland, 2014

It's a long drop to the sea
Or an impossible climb to the top.
The county is Clare and you
Think of John Clare, another
Poet. He had a difficult life
With insanity building up
Like these cliffs with 320 million
Years of mud as the pre-historic
River moved in slow motion
Out of itself.

       You can claim for yourself
The salt and the water, tears
Of unchartered seas and those
Lost survivors, like yourself
Holding tight to whatever will
Not move. You can live with
The craziness of your rage
Against the waves breaking
Down your fighting spirit.

    Watch carefully how the sea works.
Relentless with its pounding heart
She comes into the bay
Of stones, rushes the wall
And backs off for breathing
Time until someone like John Clare

Or you, dying and writing poems
Stirs the waters with mud
Coming out of itself as if to escape
Once more from the asylum.
Swim, swim hard before you come
Out of yourself after all these millions
Of years. Swim from wall to wall.
You are crazy once more, in love.

SCOTTISH WATER

You move in a way that
draws those watching along
like one wave behind another.
It's the sea coming into
the gently sloped cove,
the arms of centuries old
caress and kiss. It's the mouth
of the ancient rescue at the edge
of everything being lost. Your life
steals a glance over your shoulder,
your hair much longer than before
and golden, ready to be spun by
the expert and grateful lover, one
wave gliding in, then one more.

YOU MUST HAVE YOUR FAMINE

You shout to the North Sea
From the Scottish coast.

You tear the skin from
The largest rock older

Than our talk of love
Creating all this water.

There comes a time when
You must have your

Famine, your war, domestic
Dangers. You shout

At the North Sea
And your words come back

To remind you of the storm
And that love battering

The ancient wall of warriors
Slashed into tiny pieces.

On the legs of salt
Created for you to survive

You shout at her
And she becomes the mist.

You shout, you swim until
The ice in the sea holds you still
With lust and very, very hungry.

SCOTTISH PRAYER BOOK

You've stopped for the night
And the headstrong
Dreams come in
Fighting for attention
Like the waves crashing
Against the white and black rock.
You get up quickly
To go stand
In the middle of the street.
You scream some inaudible words,
So help you God, in a prayer
For the hand around your heart,
Inside your cage of ribs,
Trying to bring you back to life.

SCRAPE

LIES I'VE HEARD OR TOLD

I love you.

I hate you.

We are now out of Iraq.

There are WMD's in Iraq so we must invade.

No, there isn't someone else.

Yes, you get the children as often as I do.

We've landed on the moon.

Algebra is easy.

I was at the library studying.

You're making this into something it's not.

You have beautiful legs.

I don't miss my dead parents.

You look twenty years younger than that.

You look ten years younger than him.

You look great!

The bottled water is better for you than tap.

I feel great!

Every joint in my body hurts.

Yes, you get the children as often as I do.

Trust me.

REVENGE

Never mind. The next week
Will tell the story. We can
Then find our way onto the right
Road, smother our path with oil
And white flour. You are a danger
To yourself, a gift to others.
Always giving your number
So they'll have someone to
Talk to, any time of day or night.
The sunflower is such a signal,
Like a lighthouse at the edge
Of the world. You hold on to
The stalk, the glimpse of a cloud,
Wait for the giant wave to lunge
In beautiful revenge against your stone.

WEEDS

Hers is one of those really
sad and exhausting lives.
The weeds are growing wild
and blue. There is a simple
and straightforward song,
something that explains it all.
Hers was one of those really
sad and exhausting lives.

LEARNING TO RIDE

In the second grade in Northwest Kansas in your small town,
You were learning to ride your bicycle. You pedaled along
The sidewalk gliding past large trees between you and the street.
You also had a "rice crispy treat" secured by unreliable but
Helpful teeth for the moment. It was a quiet day, most likely
A Sunday afternoon. You became distracted or just lost your
Balance both of which you have done many times since. Then
You hit one of those large trees straight on stopping the bike
But not you. You landed on the ground, sat up, pulled the "treat"
Out of your mouth along with some pink saliva and a previously
Loose tooth. You were lucky. It was 1952, your father was trying
To stay alive fighting a war in Korea, earning a couple of Bronze
Stars for bravery, while you were trading secrets with the "enemy,"
As your mother would say, but whom you describe to friends as
The cute Methodist minister's blond daughter very willing to share.

PUTTING DOWN

How she withstood
His care, aware
Or not. It will
Always be a question
For me. It always
Will seem more like
Treatment than care.
Or mistreatment.
Maybe a love song
Gone terribly wrong.

THE FLAPPER BIRD

There are so many ways to speak
Your heartache and give voice
To the tired and lonely blood
Flowing from the mattress out into
The hallway. The freedom fighters
Had no idea of what the
Blood would look like, so red
And life-soaked into UNESCO
Treasures. Those who survived
To tell the story do it every
Chance they get. Grease the
Gears, barely ask the question
And the bird beats the wings
Into remission, the breath
Tasting like her tongue excited
To enter the love of her life.

PHRASING

My body is not working
So good today.
Not good.
Not well.
Pick your phrase
While I go to the bathroom
Again.

HEADLINES

2016 to be year of fear
in U.S. I did not read
the article but I suppose
it could be many things:
Presidential race, Middle East,
gun violence, Planned Parenthood,
immigration, 400 families
versus the rest of us, police shootings,
the death penalty, incarceration,
so many possibilities. We don't fight
over the best poems or the worst.
Or at least that conflict never makes
Headlines. Think of that: Doty
Slips up in twelfth debate with Nye.
Primary in Iowa now leaning toward Urrea.
Nation undecided over next poetic leader.

GIVE IT YOUR ALL

I am skipping the tragic parts.
Even so there is enough
Bad news to at least give the good
A dash for the penny.

Talk into the mirror and give
It your all. But, you complain,
I did that yesterday. What?
I ask. Gave it my all, you reply.

You agree that the accumulated
Dead from centuries of war mean nothing.
I said I would skip the tragic
But then I glanced back over my shoulder.

SOMETHING TO HIDE: A SONNET

Do you have something against light?
The blinds and curtains
Are always closed
Until I open them
Sometimes not until noon.
Are you hiding something
From the world outside?
Or hiding something from

Me? Because either way
It's not working. I can
Tell when the world has
Caught on to your tricks.
As for me, I've seen your love
Between us for years in bed.

GOOD FRIDAY, AGAIN

I know I ask too many
Questions but how can
I learn and move on if
I keep silent at the back of
The room. I will cook my
Last meal myself, sneak
Into the press room to hear
Directly the latest news,
Rumors of war, the edge
Of bloodshed.

Tonight I could smell the
Out of control wildfire,
Biggest in the history of Kansas
That we know of, evacuating
Towns, burning the ranches
Within reach, the cattle clustered
Under exploding trees when they
Could have waded into the ponds
For safety. With all this news
I noticed you have the laugh
Of someone in love. I will cook my
Last meal before the betrayal.
Curious, that laugh. Mocking me
For not seeking safety in the water.

SCRAPE

As you get older
Your skin becomes
Less, not more, calloused.
Your consciously thick
Skin is disappearing
Layer by layer. You scrape
Your hand or arm
In a slight, careless
Way, and the blood
Quickly appears
Opening you to all
Possibilities of the day ahead.

CANDLE

Forty years ago
I put the car in reverse,
looked straight ahead
through the windshield
and saw the light,
a candle in her window.
I had come to say goodbye
at 3 a.m. I was crazy
in my first love and losing
the dream. In a few hours
I would be driving east,
away from the Pacific,
far away from the sea.
I don't remember what we
said. I do remember not
making love, ever, still.
I drove away, lost and weary,
longing for the bridled fear
to free the tongue, for the
courage to stay and help
her blow out the candle.
We would then watch
the smoke climb the wall,
we would never be
broken again, or fall.

DAILY PAPER

I have arranged my interior
furniture so you have a very
special place to reside in
my heart. I hope that's ok.
Let me know if that's not safe
for you. I don't want you to
feel trapped or made to take
up residence in an inappropriate
neighborhood. Trash pick up
is Thursday, daily paper tossed on porch.
Good hot water for our showers. I'll be happy
to fix anything for you.

SALT

Even the score
before the tide turns
and you find
the sunset crawling
up your back
down your front
like the hands
of water ripping
and churning in circles
sending you out
toward the vast
sweet current
tasting like fruit
you sprayed over
your body
and the salt
that preserved
you for me forever.

THE OVER-RIPE SUN

The over-ripe sun
is taking its time to find a lost sea
among all the missing
and presumed drowned bodies of
water. It is taking a step
in unknown territory
only because it is so ripe.
Otherwise it would never have the courage.
It will take a long time,
more than you care to wait.
Even if there is a good chance
it will quench your thirst,
bathe you into wholeness.

WE WANT TO BE BETTER OFF

Those you see on the screen
are the lucky ones, they
at least have some debris
to work with. Splinters of
two by fours, broken
PVC pipe, various sheets
of plywood for a roof.
Those you don't see
on the screen are the unlucky
ones. They are under the mud,
their gravesites now the foundation
for this new village. No one
wants to talk to us, standing
as we are on their buried
families. [Sorry it has been
so long in this empty search] You,
he said, are not helping with your
words, microphones, and cameras.
We want to be better off.
Find your own red mud-slide
then try being photogenic.

DEEP, LIKE AN OLD MOVIE

It will be fine.
I will sleep my deprivation
away very soon. All the craving
hangs from my arms
like apples on a tree. It all
runs deep like an old movie
about a submarine. The deeper
the more pressure on the hull, the skin
so exposed, any slight fracture
will split open causing major
damage and certain loss
on the ocean floor.

The children will make a wreath
of paper, glue and glitter
to welcome us home as heroes.
They will wait, arms aching
to lift us, their loved ones missing
at sea, a deprivation they will learn
to live with as the waves crash around them
crushing the sand into glass.

Michael Poage was born in Virginia and has lived and worked in New England, California, Montana, Kansas and overseas in Latvia, Palestine, Mexico, Gaza and Bosnia and Herzegovina. He has twelve books of poems published prior to this new book. He worked various jobs before becoming ordained in the United Church of Christ and serving three congregations in Kansas. He has also taught at Friends University, Wichita State University, the University of Latvia and Dzemal Bijedic University in Mostar, Bosnia and Herzegovina, where he also served as Poet-in-Residence, 2017-18. When not in Bosnia and Herzegovina, he and his wife, the historian and writer, Dr. Gretchen Eick, live in Wichita, Kansas.